at the eleventh hour

Elizabeth Beech

Gothic Image Publications
7 High Street, Glastonbury,
Somerset BA6 9DP

© Elizabeth Beech 1995

Typeset Michael Mepham, Frome Somerset
Printed and bound in Great Britain by
Wincanton Print Ltd, Somerset

Cover photograph by the author: Stokes Croft, Bristol, 1995

All rights reserved. No part of this publication may be
reproduced or utilised in any form or by any means
without written permission from the Publisher

A catalogue record for this book is available
from the British Library

ISBN 0 906362 33 4

FOREWORD

I have two interpretations of the phrase the eleventh hour.
I occasionally say "at the eleventh hour....", by which I mean,
"at the last moment", or "just in time" or "almost too late".
I was made aware of another meaning during my childhood.
My father explained that the ceasefire, which ended the First
World War, was timed to take place on the eleventh hour of
the eleventh day of the eleventh month.

It was only when I chose the phrase as the title of this work
that I looked for its origin. I discovered that the words come
from the New Testament parable of the vineyard, as rendered
by Matthew, (20.V9.-16). In the parable workers have been
hired early in the morning to do a day's work for a day's pay
but, "at the eleventh hour", more workers are hired, who do
one hour's work. When the time comes for payment, the
labourers who have worked all day are paid a day's wage, as
are those who have worked for an hour. Those who were
hired first complain bitterly, but the vineyard owner tells them
that they agreed to the terms of their employment, and that
the owner has a right to do what he wants with what belongs
to him.

We are told at the start of the parable that this is what the
kingdom of heaven is like. We are told at the end that "...the
last will be first, and the first will be last."

This is one of several gospel stories which challenge my
assumptions about justice, reward and punishment, blame
and judgement, and perhaps more importantly, the possible
meaning of the word equality.

Elizabeth Beech
Glastonbury, October 1995

A special thank you to Gillian Booth for her support for my work, and to Frances Howard-Gordon, whose sensitive editing, and commitment to this project enabled *at the eleventh hour* to be published.

PROLOGUE

When I look back on family celebrations in the aftermath of the Second World War I remember the excitement of the ceremonial opening of the large parcel sent by my mother's brother from Australia. It always contained souvenirs, from the small sheep farming town in New South Wales to which my uncle had emigrated long before I was born.

My father was of the opinion that everyone was somehow involved in producing these tasteless items, inscribed with the name of this obscure town in the middle of nowhere, since everyone in the town was an immigrant who wanted to send gifts home which announced that the spot on the planet that they had chosen to settle was worthy of the same note as Blackpool or the Tower of London, as indeed, to us, they were. These presents were treasured, despite their incongruity amongst the Rockingham china and Stuart crystal in our family home.

My picture of the other side of the world was profoundly influenced by all this. I had an image of a town, just like those in Wild West films, with one main street, surrounded by a featureless plain, inhabited by sheep, and men on horses, and a large wooden building in which people worked at producing these mugs, and tea towels, and key rings.

Almost forty years later, my brother went to New South Wales to work, and our family celebrations were excited by a phone call from him. We always remarked on how clear the line was, "You could be down the road!" and how odd it was to imagine him the other side of the world, eating Christmas lunch yesterday, or is it tomorrow?

"Is it Boxing Day over there?"

on the beach in hot summer sun, and, whatever he said, I found it impossible to change my fixed idea, formed in my childhood, of what that region of Australia was like. My imagination, fuelled by scraps of information, was a more potent force than mere facts, however proven.

So I think the boundaries between fact and fiction are blurred and, as a consequence, honest remembering has almost nothing to do with the truth, as in "I swear by Almighty God to tell the truth, the whole truth and nothing but the truth".

This creates a paradox

what I say is true

and yet

"You can't most always generally tell"

as my Gran, so often said.

Kitty Barter, who lived in our house in a room which smelt of lavender water and Devon violets, and whose walls were covered with pictures of cottages with roses round the door, and crinoline ladies, and 'sayings'.

"If you see the funny side
you'll walk along the sunny side
while other folk are walking in the rain"

"Telling the truth makes you safe"

said Sister Louis Gabriel, who wore shoes with heels, and spat as she spoke in her thick accent, terrifying us with her passion and conviction. Sister Louis Gab, who later metamorphosed into Charlotte Klein, German, Jewish Catholic nun, in a bright red dress, smoking cigarettes and alarming and charming my children as she had alarmed and charmed me all those years before.

Women as different as two people can be.

Apparently,
at opposite ends of the spectrum;

dark and light

sunshine and rain.

the rainbow

the covenant.

the promise,

and the promise is 'good', or 'happy ever after', although I don't quite know what the promise is.

When I walked through the gates at Birkenau I had no idea what I would discover

Or any thought of what I was looking for.

It was partly a pilgrimage for these two women, or a thanksgiving for their lives, and also a journey to lay my past to rest.

I found a place which described the human condition.

Gaudy hot house flowers, lovingly presented by other pilgrims, vied, uneasily, with the grasses and trees which have pushed through the stern concrete.

Little plastic 'Star of David' flags flapped hopefully against the rusty wire.

Children invented games to play on the wooden sleepers of the notorious railway line which runs relentlessly through the centre of the site.

The World Monument was an edifice which looked destined to last for at least another millennium, while the red brick gateway, through which a million victims passed, seemed ready to crumble to dust.

I sat under some birch trees and weaved a dream of planting there, the most beautiful garden on earth.

Eden.

Our promise. The promised land.

The covenant we make,

"Never again will I curse the ground because of man, however evil his inclinations may be from his youth upwards. I will never again kill every living creature as I have just done.

> While the earth lasts
> seedtime and harvest, cold and heat
> summer and winter, day and night,
> shall never cease."

Genesis 8. 21.22.

you say to me

but

it's all the same it's all the same
the felling of trees
destroys us as surely as bombs

and I say

quite so
in my head I agree

but I tell you my friend
as well

that a tree is
a fire
a table
a raft

and you can't most always generally tell

but

a man or
a woman or
child
hacked down

that's hell

To find a way.

If I am going to protest about the felling of a tree I have to find a way to make a tree important to people who have never thought about such things before.

I have to use my imagination. It's a creative act. It's theatre, or poetry, or art, or music. Nothing else moves.

Politics don't move. Politics are based on illusions of fact. Cause and effect.

Consequences.

Art has to suspend an idea of consequences. Without that it is craft. Applied. The known. Certain. I apply a certain idea with a certain outcome. Art is risky. If it's going to work. To move. To change.

I need distance and I need closeness.

I need to hold the gaze in a world of short attention spans.

I need to create a make believe that is believable.

I say:

"This isn't true, as in a fact. This is what I have seen. I don't even want it to be true."

It's because I don't want it to be true that I am doing this,

but

and here's the rub

unless I can give you the sense that it is true, it will, I fear, be true,

here we go round the mulberry bush.

I grew up in a world of platform tickets, porters, bus conductors "Move along please", who punched a hole in your cardboard ticket.

A world of rationing. Where a banana was a rarity. Where people said "Sir" and "Guv" and "Madam"

A world of the radio - Jean Metcalfe. Two-Way Family Favourites "for Corporal Jones B.F.P.O. Box....." What did BFPO mean? Donald Peers "Wakey Wakeeeeeeeeee" de de de der derrrrr

polished leather shoes and knitted swimming costumes, dresses with smocking and cardigans

"It's television's done it" said Granny grimly. "No-one's listening any more".

"What's a nice woman like you doing here" says the young policeman at Greenham.

A nice young woman, reared on cowboy films. Wells Fargo. She Wore a Yellow ribbon. Oklahoma, Carousel.

People will say we're in love

the second world war

Sister Louis Gabriel. A German Jewish Catholic nun "you won't forget, you war babies, you won't forget. I'm sure of that"

Auschwitz Hiroshima

we pay our debt around the fire at Greenham

that's what a nice woman like me is doing here

bandstands
de dum de dum de dum de dum here comes the galloping
major
stay in line
heads up
shoulders back
God Save Our Gracious King
all stand
God save our noble king
the Royal Tournament
God save our King
'"Hark the Herald Angels Sing"
Mrs Simpsons pinched our king',
sang my father,
what did that mean?

men raising their hats,
men wearing hats
women in scarves wrapped like turbans, and pinnies
10 minutes Mrs Whiteside
The Dambusters March
Colonel Bogey
discipline
courage
loyalty
chilblains
Owbridges
Chemical Food
Food office orange juice in medicine bottles with blue labels
food parcels from Australia

Lyons Corner House. Fullers Tea Rooms. Schoolfriend. Girl.
Enid Blyton. Nigger brown coats and grey woollen socks with
wide black elastic garters that made marks on your legs and
cut off your circulation
the Hungarian revolution
rock and roll
ITV
colour
light

who rolled away the grey, the brown, the dirty yellow?

It just went away
-click-
that world that had lasted in a steady continuum
all gone
all changed
remember remember
Auschwitz,
Hiroshima,
Hungary,
Vietnam,
Biafra,
Cambodia,
Ethiopia,

The ticket inspector says;

"It's stopping for people to get on"

"Well, if they're getting on can't I get off? I asked at the ticket office, they said it was stopping." The young woman looks desperate,

"It all depends. It's not a scheduled stop"

We all start laughing "But if people are getting on, can't she get off", we say,

"It all depends" he says firmly.

What does it depend on?

Someone saying it's all mad.

"I said to him" yells a taxi driver to another, "I said to him you must be fucking joking",

and a woman, who reminds me of my grandmother, struggles along in a powder blue coat which matches her hair, dragging her luggage on two tiny wheels, which catch in the polystyrene trays, and plastic wrappers, which waft and settle on the station forecourt like scavengers.

"Fucking joking", he repeats at increased volume, as his mate revs his engine.

"They're all fucking bastards" says the smart young woman to her friend across the table, as I settle in the seat next to her,

"Still, lucky really, if I hadn't been pregnant I'd have got six months. She asked for it. They said I stabbed her. Fucking wankers. God, this is a boring journey," she concludes, as the train starts.

Perhaps I am nice after all
sugar and spice and all things nice,

as the sun breaks through and we trundle past the gardens that back the track with their reassuring lines of washing

Imagine

Imagine

all you need is love der de der de der
all you need is love de der de der der

all you need is love love, love is all you need.

and I blow my nose again

and again

and again

and then I stop, because it feels as though I could blow my nose forever. As if there's something up my nose which cannot be blown away however much I huff and puff

a badness

a disease

of course this is just a physical ailment, nothing to do with anything to do with this

there's just a lot of it about and I've got it. It's nothing more or less than that

my what a fuss some people make

"you're very bunged up" they say on the phone

"yes", I say, "I am"
"well, hope you'll feel better soon"

which I will,

when it gets colder

when the weather gets harder and this grey, warm drizzle stops

the bugs are still biting, though it's November, and moulds are growing

it all needs killing off by a sharp frost, a good cold spell

like cold showers, recommended for lust,

we think everything is joined up, and then we separate it all. We say it's all connected, and then we decide it isn't

Great surging hormones, biological urgings. We think that means sex, we think we know what we want, but do we know what we want when we want...

"don't stop, don't stop" she says

so he doesn't and then it's alright for a bit, or it's better than if he had stopped because then she wouldn't have been sure, perhaps he didn't like her, or find her attractive, or wouldn't stay with her

women want people to stay with them

women want to have the choice to let people go

women don't like being let go of

don't stop, don't go

I've let you in, I won't let you out

you won't go 'till I say so

come into my parlour said the spider to the fly

do men know women are like this?

is it all just an extension of a game, a dare

a game

get in

get out

see if you can

I dare you

you won't have to be there long

you just get there and come back

you climb up Everest and you put a flag in the top and have your photograph taken and then you come down again

you did it

you conquered it

what did you conquer?

did it shift and groan

did it notice or care?
did it express pleasure? does that matter as long as you did it

did Everest hold you, and rock you and make you feel safe and warm and if it didn't, what was it for except capture and conquest.

He's sitting on the floor, pulling at the wire on the microphone. The wire is getting tighter and tighter. The singer doesn't notice. I notice. But I'm too far away.

His mother emerges from behind the bar. Can in hand. She goes over to talk to some men at a distant table. He pulls the wire tighter still. Surely the whole lot is going to topple over, stand, microphone and all. Still no-one seems to notice. Why don't they see? If I point it out it will interrupt the singer. Maybe his mother will notice. Where is his mother? I can't even see her now.

He looks around and sees that no-one sees. He starts twitching at the wire, then lets it fall a little. Loosens the tension and starts swinging it. Rocking it.

I hear his mother's shrill high laugh, right at the back of the room. Laughing. Too loudly. I turn towards the sound. She stands there. Swaying slightly to the music. Hand on hip, elbow nudging towards the man in the chair, Come on, teases the elbow. Come on, you look game for a laugh.

He swings on the wire. He's six. Maybe eight. Big six, little eight. I don't know. Whatever. He should be tucked up in bed.

Bye baby bunting
Mummy's gone a hunting

When the bough breaks
the cradle will fall
down will come cradle
baby
and all

We start by groping and fumbling on park benches, in the backs of cars, on wet grass - this is England after all - and most of us have brief moments of perfumed glamour - the tinkle of ice in glasses, the stroking of limbs, until we face the reality of farting and flab and a sense of shame at the prospect of nakedness more profound than any adolescent angst.

The wretched drunken men who leer out of doorways, flies undone, speaking in a measured caricature of half remembered movie sequences

"Good morning ma'am", he says, raising an imaginary hat, "could you spare me twenty pee?"

No, not one, good sir, you've enough of your own dribbling across my path, mingling with the beer you have just spilt

and he retreats into the shadows to rehearse another scene as I step daintily over the foaming liquid encircling the dog turds.

"Gentlemen always walk on the outside", informs my father, "to stop the horses splashing the ladies skirts."

We are walking along a seafront, just after the second world war. I'm on the inside, the sea side. The milkman has a horse, it must be that. My father raises his hat to people as they pass. He wears leather gloves.

Is this comedy or tragedy? "Where do gentlemen walk now, Daddy?" Inside or outside or do they all drive cars, and pick up the ladies waiting outside Marks and Spencers with their bottles of water, with a hint of peach, a dash of lime; and who pay with cards that swoosh through grooves on the till

"Spare any change?", says the young man wrapped in a sodden blanket, just outside the automatic door,

only the poor have change,

only the poor have cash.

My gran said red and white flowers together symbolised death
my friend says she thought it was about the wars of the roses
it all goes back a long way
all over England guys are burnt once a year
and we chant

remember, remember the fifth of November
                      gunpowder, treason and plot
and no-one says Catholic plot,
or mentions that the gunpowder was sold by the State to trap the plotters,

anymore than we talk much about the arms trade that forms a major part of our economic stability,

such as it is,

or that we'll sell these arms to anyone, more or less
                  nudge, nudge,
                  wink, wink,
better not to ask too many questions, eh.,?

The diamond cartels mining in the heat of Africa
did deals with the diamond traders in the frost of Siberia
during the hot part, of the cold war,
which we won
on the strength of:

hamburgers, rock music, satellite tv, videos,

you thought it was about ideology,

sorry, my dear,

it was about greed.

My friends and I discuss the merits of Native American
ceremonies to empower our lives. It's funny what we talk
about at the end of the twentieth century
funny peculiar not funny ha-ha.

We talk about astrology, numerology, crop circles,
aromatherapy.
homeopathy,
we have cures for this, and cures for that,

try this or that, we shout as we wave a friend off in a car,
chugging blue fumes at the exact level of the mouth and nose
of an infant being trundled along in a buggy.
"I'm going to Relaxation," says a friend, yawning," it's only six
quid". She lays her head on the table. " God I'm tired".

Isn't it cheaper to go to bed?

I think of relaxing ways to spend six quid

A bottle of wine
perfume   bath oil   flowers,

a trip to the cinema and a bar of chocolate,

a trip to London on the bus.

Greed won,

there are no cures for what ails us.

I was often bored, or if not exactly bored I suffered from a feeling of not knowing what to do, or not wanting to do the things which had been proscribed - Sunday afternoon walks in biting cold winds, tidying my room, doing jig-saw puzzles, playing board games, or cards.

Daily life had an inexorable pattern. Even the food was predictable; joint on Sunday, cold meat Monday, (washday,) mince on Tuesday, and so on. Salads were for summer; lettuce, cucumber, tomato with Heinz salad cream. Parsnips, swedes, turnips in the winter. Food was delivered by milkmen, bakers, butchers, fishmongers, grocers. We hardly went shopping, except for clothes and shoes, twice a year. Furniture and linen and china and glass and cutlery were inherited, not bought.

My father had a wind-up gramophone which played 78's. Jessie Mathews, Sousa marches, operettas and a medley of extracts from Hollywood films of the 30's and 40's. My father's film magazines, all muted and silver, glamorously nestled my mother's stack of 'Theatre World'.

Childhood took a long time, in the 1940's and 50's. The space between Christmas' was immeasurable, vast.

Time hurtles by now.

People used to say that time goes faster when you are older, but even the children are saying they can't believe it's nearly Christmas again, already.

This year it's CD Rom's, modems for computers to hook you into the information super highway. Interactive TV. Not a moment to be bored.

"I'm bored" says a child with a ten minute gap between swimming and ballet. "See if there's anything on TV then." Pick up the remote control, put, put, put, put, put, put, flick through the channels, clicking the buttons, hardly glancing at the screen, "No, nothing, there's absolutely nothing on. Can we get a video after ballet? Oh, I got my certificate today", and the child rummages in her rucksack, scattering little cardboard cartons with straws, and a miniature woman with disproportionately large pointy breasts and silver blonde hair, and rainbow coloured pens that write in neon, and, eventually, pulls out a piece of paper. 'The Run for Life' it blazes boldly, and informs that this diminutive child has covered many sponsored miles to feed the children of Africa.

The walls of her room are plastered with similar achievements. This child has done huge deeds for: whales, dolphins, rainforests, orphans in Eastern Europe, dogs, cats, caged and uncaged species of every variety, including human,

this child has saved the world, over and over again, in the course of her life, which has been in existence for less than a decade.

What must it be like to do these things? To put all your energy and effort into these vast rescue operations as if you were to blame, as if it was your fault, as if it were up to children now to salvage our planet at

three minutes to midnight,

the eleventh hour,

the last minute.

"Come on, time for ballet. We're too late to walk, we'll have to go in the car. Come on. Hurry up. Oh do get a move on".

When I think of England I think of cricket, rugby, football, soldiers, the Church of England, public schools, pubs, trade unions, lager louts and hooray Henry's. I think of masculine culture.

Women swim in and out of view............

Queen Victoria, Emmeline Pankhurst, Virginia Woolf, Margaret Thatcher....

individual women,

groups of men.

Women together are regarded with suspicion unless they're doing something useful - like nurses, or the WI.

The suffragettes, like the women's liberation movement, described with accuracy the aspirations of women, but both were deemed 'too strident' to be accepted with any confidence.

"Oh no" say women dressed in jackets with padded shoulders, on their way to the Stock Exchange or the Bar, "I'm not a feminist"."What?" say the young women in their Doc Marten's, and shaven heads "oh no, I'm not interested in all that".

There was one moment in our history when, for a spell, England was feminine.

On December 12, 1982, more than 30,000 women from all over the British Isles, gathered outside an air-base near Newbury, Berkshire.

Conservative, Liberal and Labour women. Catholic and Protestant women. Black women and white women. Old and young. Upper class, middle class, working class. Just women.

Nobody expected it. We didn't expect it ourselves. It was a surprise. Two coach loads of women came from our little market town. As we drove towards the site, coach after coach after coach converged creating a vast, happy traffic jam. We didn't care if we didn't arrive, the journey became as important as the destination. We sang, we laughed, we waved to each other through the windows of our buses. We recognised each other. Women. Just women.

We did, in fact, arrive. Wave upon wave of us. For the biggest gathering of women this country has ever seen. We were there to put an end to war. We were going to do it by embracing the base, and embrace the base we did.

It was on the front page of every newspaper in the country, the news spread all over the world, and Greenham Common became.

A dream came true that day, and fears of a commitment to change petering out through lack of interest were eradicated, but we were unprepared for the real meaning of our statement.

We wanted an end to war. We said that for centuries men had left home for war and now women were going to leave home for peace. We invoked our heroines for inspiration "We will best make the world we want not by using your ways and methods but by finding new ways and making new methods" our posters said. We meant every word of it. Innocent of the magnitude of the task, and our own hypocrisies.

We were women.

We were different.

Men wanted war.

Women wanted peace.

Simple.

I thought.

"Leave me alone to get on with it."

We have the answer. We are the solution. You are the problem. Not all of you, but most of you.

Women are different.

By different, at that time, I meant better. I didn't say better, and, probably, if anyone had asked me, I would not have said better. I would have fudged about, and talked about conditioning, and the fact that women were fortunate in many ways because, by being kept back, kept at home, they were not as vulnerable to the rules of the system. I would have said that men were more damaged by patriarchy than I was because they were more involved with it than I was. I would have talked about the personal being the political and that is what women are good at, better at. And probably you wouldn't have argued with me that much. I would have said it quite politely. I was a peace woman after all. I saw things as black and white. It was a matter of making a decision. Either/or. For war, or for peace. I didn't realise we are all killers and that there are many, many ways to make war.

I went to Greenham to make peace.

At Greenham I discovered the seeds of war.

There are rumors in esoteric circles about the appearance of a second sun in the sky, and the changes this happenstance will bring about. People thrill to the idea of a cosmic upheaval which will provide an answer.

Armageddon or the Messiah.
Either way we abdicate responsibility.

The work, the sheer work involved is too daunting.
Better a second sun,
better not think about the reality of this though,

oceans rising,
temperatures soaring
light blinding,

the second sun has, perhaps, arrived already

August 6 1945

didn't you notice?

It is said that our ancestors didn't know that men were necessary to create life. Women gave birth and were reverenced for this capacity, awe full significance was given to their connection to nature. To the moon. Were women pleased when it was realised that men were crucial to this creative process? That without them there would be no human life.

Can we go back back then and imagine this. Do we all know everything which is known?

I try to imagine unknowing. I try to imagine not realising about men.

What did they do all day? What were they for?

Sexual pleasure and certain sort of jobs I suppose

like the hive. No function but to serve the queen, and the whole.
Busying about. Coming up with ideas to relieve the aching futility. The sense of nothingness

Men invented the death machines and their greatest invention is, the ultimate death machine

the atomic bomb.

The women bring life and
the men bring death.

Which is better?
Life or death?

Do you know the answer to this?
truly, do you know the answer?

Or are you still deciding?

Is it better to bring life or to bring death?

and what does this mean?

Men bring life.

And women bring death.

As well. Too. Also. And.

August 6 1945.

We bring death to everything. We know that. The blazing of the second sun. We bring life and we bring death. We have the potential for both.

"Rejoice, rejoice" says the woman, as a ship full of conscripts is blown away. Rejoice in the hideous deaths of these young men.

"Bring back hanging" bay the women, as a young man with his head covered in a sack is bustled into court.

I flap my arm carelessly to ward off a small insect. It plummets to the floor. I go to water my balcony, late on a summer's evening . Crunch goes the shell of a snail beneath my feet.

We are all killers. To be alive is to bring death. This is a reality. This is the reality of the atomic bomb. The sharp, irrevocable consciousness that we can destroy everything. Everything. All life.

Do we nag and harry and harp on and on about it until we, the women, finally come to understand the enormity of what is being said.. ....

we, all of us,

him and her,

you and me,

have the power of life and death.

Millenia have separated these realisations. Millenia in which, like children, we looked for rescue or cruel judgement.

It's time to grow up. We have choices to make.

You think I am being soft on men.

It is said we can remember everything. Yet I have told you I can't remember when I didn't know that men, too, brought life

and then, of course, I dream

a dream

I am walking. There is no landscape. It is colour, deep grey, maroon. It is texture like opaque velvet. I look down and on the ground is a body. It is the body of a man, with his face destroyed. His face is hideous. His face is pustules and weeping, suppurating sores. His features are obliterated by damage and decay.

I know I must carry this man. So I pick him up, and I place his body over my shoulder, so his head hangs down and rests on a place on my back, below my shoulder blades, where my lungs are. I glance around, and there, to my left is a huge staircase, and I know I must carry the man up the staircase, the top of which I cannot see. I carry him up. His weight is not burdensome but the carrying is a drudgery. His head bangs and bangs thud..thud..thud..against my back. It feels like a large, soft, rubber ball. Not uncomfortable. The rhythm does not match my own.

It is a very long climb.
It needs stamina
not strength.
It is nothing.
Nothing changes.

After so long I reach the top.
It is lighter here,
though there is no colour to remember.

I know I must now lay the body down.
I put my hands around his waist and,
as I do so,
he springs from my grasp.
Springs and leaps away from me, and stands,
laughing.

His face is utterly restored.
He is beautiful.
I don't know what he looks like.

I feel such pleasure that even on waking the feeling stays with me.

Each time I remember this dream.

and you think there are reasons for this too.

Electrical impulses in the brain.
Secret, unacknowledged sexual desire.
You think this is a sexual fantasy.
Or you think this is about my father.
Or my mother.
But how can you be sure?

You think things that don't make sense.
Or perhaps you try not to bring them to thought.
Do you tell anyone these things,
or do you keep quiet?
The fear runs very deep.

You will not be believed.

If you are not believed you will go mad.

The fear of madness is always there.
Every family has its share.

Are you 'just like' some member of your family you have never met - a lunatic, a deviant, a dotty aunt, an obscene uncle.

We trace our histories for clues.
We look for explanations

we gather round fires and share our stories

women

men

women don't remember riding into battle
men don't remember nursing babies

but women remember using weapons
and men remember cradling the bodies of their fallen
comrades

you say I am soft on men,
hard on women.

I am a woman.
Hard.
Hardness.

Love is hard.
Love is the hardest thing I'll ever do.

Look at it all,
just look at it.

Will it get better if I hate?

Will it get better if I blame?

I try to understand.
I try so hard to understand.

"Have you got a cigarette?" says the young woman standing on the corner.

It's 1 am on a cold night. She's standing with her arms wrapped across her breasts, feet stamping on the pavement shod in long white plastic high heeled boots. Her tiny skirt just reaches the top of her thighs. Her skimpy jumper dips to her waist.

"No. I've got a roll up though"

"Could you do it. I'm hopeless at rolling" she says. Her fingers are too cold anyway.

As I roll I say

"OK tonight?"

"Slow", she says. "One more and I'm off. A quick blow job will do nicely. I can score then"

I hand her the roll up

"Ta. What your name?" I tell her, and where I live.

"Look, just over there. See that window. That's my place, come for a cuppa sometime"

"Would you really be my friend?"

"Yes" I say "I would".

I want to take her home. I want to give her a cup of tea. A bath. A clean towel. Clean sheets. A hot water bottle. I want her to use my bath oil. I want her to eat scrambled eggs. I want her to feel safe. I want her not to give anyone a blow job ever again. I want her not to have this job at all.

I want her to be loved.

Men say they think about sex all the time.

When we were children, playing, you could shout Pax to get out of the game if it got too rough, or you got tired, or even bored.

"Pax" I would shout. A stitch in my side. Bending over double and panting.

And the others would leave me alone.

Pax means peace.

This will not stop if we go on blaming and judging.

The house is on fire.
I don't know who started the fire.
Some say this thing and some say that thing.

Back and back we go,
trying to find out.

Will it make any difference when
we know who's fault it was?

Adam
or Eve
or the serpent.
Which are you?

If we want it to stop we could try shouting

PAX.

I read the correct translation of The Frog Prince last night. The princess did not restore the prince with a kiss. She found his frog form so repulsive that she "dashed him against the wall with all her might", and as he fell to the floor he transformed into a king's son with beautiful smiling eyes.

I go down the street. Sitting propped against a wall is a man, he's maybe thirty. He holds a can in his hand. Between his legs is a stream of piss he has created, snaking down the pavement towards me. He raises his head and makes these noises at me "grrrrrrr here grrrrrrrr come here........grrrrrrrrrrrrrrr here grrrrrrrrrrr
           here come on darling...grrrr"

I walk on, stepping over his urine.

These are everyday occurrences.

Some days it feels unbearable.

Impossible.

This man was once upon a time....

We are brought up with fairy stories. We are brought up to believe things which aren't true. We are told that in the end we will live happily ever after. We think that when we are grown up somehow it will all come right. We will be cared for, protected, cherished. We will belong.

Of course it isn't like that. If I say things about how it was at Greenham it is because it is important that fairy stories are not allowed to take hold of the imagination, so that, somehow, we continue to believe in a fantasy.

Many women have been hurt in the company of women. Greenham is not unique.

People who are hurt, hurt in turn. We observe civil war, Bosnia, Rwanda, on our streets. We do it. Women do it. Terrified of separation - we have been separate so long - we cling together in like minded groupings, sects of race or creed or age or cause. We witter and gossip. We slander and libel. We point the finger - at her and her and her until we lose sight of where we started, what brought us together in the first place.

Now I feel like a fish out of water

Gasping for breath. No energy.

Books have become conventions too.

I return to the idea of messages in bottles

SOS

the writing on the wall

I want to return to the fire. To know I can stop doing this and just walk out
and there will be the fire
and the company of women.

It was difficult, but that difficulty is not as bad as this.

There is nowhere to go when I feel like this.

That's what a here and now society is like. No-one is home. Everyone is busy doing this and that. Working, or on courses, or at the dentist, or doing jobs that must be done today because life is so hectic and busy.

So that I feel like the only person in the world who has nothing to really do - except this - so I am part of the illusion. People think I'm busy and happy.

We fill our time up with things to distract from the feeling of being alone.

Shopping.
Videos.

We don't dare to think.

I don't dare to sit here much longer, watching people come and go, and imagining they are alright, when I am not, and wondering why, or how, they are alright and what's wrong with me.

There are so many words,
who needs more words?

I wanted to say something quite simple, and surely there's a way to say it in one or two sentences.

change takes place slowly

there are occasional epiphanies

and occasional disasters

but generally change evolves,

emerges,

like seasons

the rain is heavy today

"Dreadful weather again today"

"Terrible."

" At least they can't say we're having a drought. Not with all the money they're making out of water"
"We've only got ourselves to blame" "Yes. It's all those bombs we've dropped. I think something's slipped out"
"Oh well. Let's make the best of what we've got"
"That's right. Look on the bright side"

and someone puts on Ella Fitzgerald singing "Ship Without a Sail"

I grew up with war, steeped in it.

My parents knew war. They were born into war and bore their babies in war. Immediate war.
Not Yugoslavia, not Vietnam, not
safely,

over there.

Here.
Now.
Actual,
Real.

" What did you think was going to happen when war was declared?" I ask my mother.

"I thought we were going to be bombed to bits that night", she says, quite matter of fact.

What do I know of courage.

"Mummy, are the tents bullet proof?" says my infant son on the way to Greenham.

What do I know of bravery.

A plane roars overhead.
Holiday makers.
Business men.

Bombers.
Bombs about to drop.
Here.
Now.

Chaos.
Confusion.
Hell.

Any day could be your last day.

Like going to the doctor who says,

"You're on your own. There's nothing we can do. It's up to you now. You have to fight it"

Fight the fear
Somehow.
Anyhow.
Eradicate the fear.

It's not that it was jolly,
Roll out the barrel,
We'll meet again,

that's not the reason that people remember it;

it was there, every day a day of survival, a day of triumph over fear.

What frightens you?

where are you going? what are you doing with your life, what's going to happen.

Will I be happy, will I be rich, here's what she said to me..

que sera, sera, whatever will be, will be

does that mean anything now, could it have been sung at any time other than that, in the aftermath of war, in the relief from fear.

My parents have needed security ever since. Unsurprisingly,

and not too many shocks.

A woman is on television saying how angry she is about the destruction of the rainforest, and the genocide of indigenous people. She sits there, in a designer flat, Smart clothes, shiny blonde curls - wash and go o o o o

"It makes me so angry. It makes me want to murder".

Who?
who does this gorgeous young woman want to murder?

what does this feeling that she expresses firmly, if not convincingly, imply.

My parents didn't want to murder people

they were prepared,
reluctantly,
to kill

it's different
and the difference is important.

We just say things, the things we think will have an impact, but we don't mean them

and since we don't mean them
what do we mean
what have we meant since we moved away from the war zone?

This book is all written in my head. I write it all the time and come up with phrases that would surprise and astonish you. In my head it works out very well. It's moving and connects at the same time. It never stays still.

Here, slowing down, to get it down, interrupts the possibility of saying what I think.

Here are some things to ponder:

120 GP's in our city have called for a reduction in traffic due to pollution from cars damaging the health of our children.

Millions of people have bought lottery tickets. I spent part of last night fantasising spending 4 million pounds and realised it wasn't enough to do what I wanted to do.

People under 40 know almost nothing about: history, politics, or religion.

Mother Teresa is under scrutiny because she associated with the wrong people (exploiters etc), and accepted money from them. Mother Teresa has failed to judge these people, and so is a charlatan, according to the documentary.

Why has nothing been said about the Gulf War?

Because the major part of the British arms trade is with Saudi Arabia?

British service personnel are ill. Why? We were told there weren't any chemical weapons used. What are they ill with?

In the 60's Porton Down administered LSD to service volunteers to establish if it was a suitable chemical for use in warfare.

The newspaper says that the police have seized 100 cannabis plants with a street value of around £4m.

Clearly growing cannabis plants is a better bet than the National Lottery.

The Prime Minister talks about doubling the standard of living.

more cars
more food
more clothes
more electronic equipment
more, more, more, more
how much more do you need?
how much more heat and light and food and travel do you think you could consume?
are you full up yet?
are you fed up yet?
I am doing this because I am

I'm showing you what goes on in my head

all

the

time

the information super highway

the inter net which switches on each morning, automatically, as I wake up, and like last night, won't always switch off when I go to sleep

somewhere between a rock and a hard place is where we stand, and that somewhere is a place where it is essential not to notice the rock or the hard place so glaringly apparent at the edge of our vision.

The place we stand must provide an opportunity for endless consumption without which a gnawing hunger and a desperate fear will erupt and hurtle us to one of the places we have striven to avoid

here and there

hither and thither

we must stay where we are
away from the rock away from the hard place

we build our house on sand

a huff and a puff

and I'll blow your house down

I want to scare you to life.

I want to smash your head against the wall so you'll fall to the ground and before you reach the floor you'll emerge intact, with smiling eyes.

I've tried being reasonable and it didn't work.

And out of the window, just as I write this, three children on bicycles hurtle down the one way street the wrong way, and career into the traffic on the main road. A knapsack on each back, hair flying in the wind and this time, as each time before so far, they get to the other side, as an old woman stares, hanging onto the handle of her shopping trolley and a man waves a drunken admonishment, motorists swerve and brake, hiccupping into their mobile phones, and the only sane response is proffered by a flock of pigeons clustered on the pavement eating crumbs soaring in panic to the sky

and out of the window

a young man and woman and a baby stand agitated by their car which has been boxed in by another, double parked. After consultation she goes off with the baby up the street and he starts writing a note to put on the windscreen and is trying to find ways of fixing it on, since it is one of those cars with the wipers held in a little groove on the bonnet (to prevent vandalism) and he has nowhere to place his plea, when a woman emerges. She's smartly dressed, around 60 years of age, and I can see them talking, though of course I can't hear, and she is getting quite angry with him, as if the fuss was unreasonable, and the fact of the woman and the baby is no doubt being conveyed, but she is getting very angry and gets into her car, slamming the door so he has to jump away to prevent being bashed by the door, and she revs up and reverses, very fast, and I notice another vehicle, a van this time, is also double parked, and a traffic warden ambles by...

shall I just sit here, looking out of the window, and write it all down for you. You, who don't have time to look out of windows. A day in the life of this street.

All day. Every day.
There is nothing unusual about this.

This isn't called a war zone.
It's not Bosnia, or Rwanda.
This is England.

Not such a bad place

These are the things I have done

I have shouted, argued, cried, raged.
I have gone on marches, joined groups,
written to MP's and heads of state,
signed petitions,
composed leaflets,
designed posters.

I have organised jumble sales, arranged debates. I have been on tv and radio and interviewed by journalists. I have been arrested. I have gone to prison. I have argued with barristers and solicitors and magistrates and judges. I have left the children I loved and lived in a bender and a squat. I have discussed the world with priests and nuns, feminists, misogynists, pornographers, politicians, newspaper editors. I have written poems and pamphlets. I have stood up on platforms, clutching microphones with my knees and voice shaking and had things thrown at me, and received standing ovations from thousands of people. I have fasted. I have tried to be good when I wanted to be bad, and I've been bad when I wanted to be good.

I think that guilt is a very useful feeling, and a very useless emotion.

I think all feelings are useful, and all emotions are useless.

I think we think too much, and too little.

I think that understanding paradox is important.

Sunshine and rain
shadow and light
difference
brought together
makes a rainbow
which is the covenant
after all
and I think about that when I can't understand.
When it's all confused.

Last night I watched a film, they said it was a true story,
and these men,
in Africa,
were piling people into a heap.
Men, women, children.
These people were alive.
They had wide eyes,
wide open eyes
that were alive.

They sprinkled these people with petrol, quite casually, like a Dad might to light the fire on Bonfire Night, even though he knew you shouldn't, and then they walked backwards and fired a few shots into the pile,
which of course ignited it.

Dull boom,

whoosh,

silence,

blue flames turning red

as the petrol burnt off.

I try to imagine doing that, and I can't.

They could have killed them with the guns. I know this is a stupid thing to say, as if it would make it alright, which it wouldn't, but it was the casualness and the cruelty. So I just sat there with my hand stuffed in my mouth, in confusion, and I wanted to stop the thoughts in my head which were

Is it because we colonised Africa?

Are women involved?

What's the point of trying to feed these people?

I don't like black men

Am I a racist?

Yes,
if I say that I don't like black men

No,
if I say it's normal,
functional,
sane,
to be appalled by people who sprinkle petrol on people,

or send them to gas chambers
or bury them alive in the sand,
in the desert,
or bomb them,
or plan to bomb them
or design weapons
or carry weapons
or use weapons

words are weapons
use them well
no harm
no harm

I look at the stars and the moon. The stars are scattered over the city tonight. The moon is nearly full

Is it nearly full over Africa too?

I can't remember these simple things.

I can remember a time when the music of Africa was foreign, strange, discordant. Now it is part of me

Aa uum, aa uum, aa, uumm, aa, uumm, aa, uum

the roots of rhythm,

the cradle of humanity

long, long ago,

over the hills and a long way off

I ask the moon to shine sweetly on Africa

as the hot sun sets,

and the lion lies down with the lamb.

It's not all that, of course it's not all that.

It wouldn't be bearable, all that anguish and anger and pain. The filth, the decay, the seeping, loitering, despairing stench of life gone rotten. The dying all around, the machines bleeping and whirring, the sirens sounding, the bells clanging, the growling and murmuring, the oaths and threats that are uttered by habit, by rote. The exquisite politeness that cuts like a knife and terminates all exchange. The evasions and duplicities, the daily betrayals, the co-optations and complicities. The self delusion, the illusion, the glamour and tinsel and tawdry attempt to remember, or vision, a different reality.

Of which this is one,

I go to the bakers and buy fresh croissants and stand in a friendly queue, lulled and comforted by the smell of the yeast, and the flour. I go home past the noisy cafes and brew fresh coffee and sit on a balcony rich with the smell of lilies. Warm in the sun. And the sound of the traffic changes and becomes the breaking of waves on an urban shore, and a man whistles, and a woman sings and across the road a piano is practised, well, the scales rising and falling like grateful prayers.

Two women stand on the corner, cane baskets at their feet, chatting, laughing, touching each other, lightly, from time to time, a hand on a shoulder, a pause on a wrist, as birds gather on the wide pavement, recently cleaned. A mother and child pass by, hands joined. The child skips along, repeating rhetorically, will we, won't we, will we won't we, we will, we won't, we will we won't, will we, won't we.....and her mother smiles in a moment of infinite indulgence.

I plan a meal for friends. Which cloth to put on the table. What colour of candles. The flowers, the colour and texture and taste of the food.

I write letters to my children.

I boil cotton sheets in galvanised tubs and hang them on the line to blow like benevolent flags of surrender to....

dreams scented with lemon balm and lavender.

I polish with beeswax and brasso.

I gather herbs and flowers and hang them to dry.

I sip at a glass of warm red wine.

I hold the moment

and hold it

and hold it

as if it was all there is.

Struck dumb, wordless, by the enormity of it all, and my sense of helplessness.

I say that women are blind to their own participation in the war machine, as if I had answers to the rage of men, as if it was right to say "there, there, come on, it's not as bad as all that."

When it is.

Friends say we each create our own reality, and I try to believe that, and buy an amaryllis, and beetroot (good for the liver) and a great pile of oranges, for the vitamin C, to ward off colds.

I turn on TV and see the cratered remains of a Serbian runway and their defiant leader threatening retaliation, and I want the reporter to ask him direct questions, like,"How do you justify the massacre of people, what kick does it give you, what makes it worth it. What happens in your head when you receive the reports of the deaths?".

A woman said at Greenham

"We just have to be good".

If you can't be good be careful

This isn't careful.
This is murderous carelessness.

Do I contribute by watching it, or is it by minding about it? I get confused about these things. I feel I should do something, but I don't know what to do. I can't bear the thought of all those arguments again. I am wary of women, since Greenham.

I'm cautious. It doesn't look like that. I've learnt to protect myself so it doesn't show. I want community, but don't know where to find it. How to form it.

Not since then.

It's ten years now, and I live alone, and think too much. The wall has grown higher and higher and longer and longer. I feel trapped and confused and stuck. The world rushes by. Everyone else describes bustle and rush. It's too quiet here, in my head. I must change,
I must move

The ocean is grey and vast, I cling to the raft and my body is bumped by the rise and fall of the waves backwards and forwards against the rubber. The water is warm and everywhere. There is nothing else. Just the warm consuming water and the rhythmic bump..... .bump.......bump.

I could let go, but then I would drown. The raft is all I have. Me and a raft and water.

Or call it tears, call it crying, or weeping, or mourning, in the vale of tears.
The ocean of tears.

"Hail Holy Queen, Mother of mercy;
hail our life, our sweetness and our hope"

I have a friend, she is called July. She lives up the road. She only came to see me when I was in the garden. No-one else saw her. When I go to school the nuns explain about guardian angels.

July is my guardian angel. She is the same age as me, but cleverer, and stronger, and unlike me she doesn't wear glasses.

"Dear guardian angel make me better than I've been today, because Mummy can't be doing with it."

"To thee do we send up our sighs, mouring and weeping in this vale of tears"

and the nothing becomes grief

and the grief becomes resolution, or at least calm.

The sky is a murky grey pink.

The children come home from school. Raucous fighting, chucking their rucksacks around, shouting half understood obscenities at each other. Do they go home for malt bread and mugs of milk, sitting in front of the telly to watch Playschool?

We are told not, more like an empty house and a video nastie.

For all the analysis - Marx, Freud, Jung, feminist - it still isn't clear to me what makes the difference. Nature, or nurture, or?

It seems it must be 'or', otherwise it would make sense, be clear.

I think the things I think, feel the things I feel, because of whatever this 'or' is.

The soul, the personality, the total experience.

As random as the lottery ticket numbers rolling out in our sitting rooms on a Saturday night. No rationale. No logic. Just a funfair cascade. A joke. A chance. No merit in being a winner. No shame in being a loser. Just luck. Just the wheel of fortune turning. A new meaning to someone's number being up....or?

Perhaps not. According to chaos theory, which I barely understand, there's a kind of critical mass of mess and disorder, which then becomes transformed to coherent patterns, and no-one knows why, or how, or when, especially when, the critical mass is reached.

Many millions of people have had roughly the same experience as me, but they don't think, and feel, like me. Not even my sister or my schoolfriends.

They saw the images of Belsen, Auschwitz, Hiroshima.

They were told to go to sleep each night contemplating the crucified Christ, and thinking about death.

I had an illuminated crucifix, a travesty of the neon signs at Piccadilly Circus, which glowed, faint red, two inches high, to ward off night time terrors. Or create them.

Marie Goretti was all the rage, a teenage Italian girl, who had killed herself rather than be raped. We dutifully agreed that this was the best course of action, but I privately knew that's not what I would have done.

The nuns explained transubstantiation. The body and blood of Christ made actually manifest, on the altar, at the Mass. I said," People don't really believe that, everyone would faint, especially the priests and servers who would be very near to it, and anyway, surely if it were true we wouldn't be expected to eat it." And I was sent out of the room. It was a First Communion class.

I was six years of age.

We bought Black Babies for 2/6d and baptised them in the name of our choice. Some girls bought lots, because their mothers would give them the money. My mother would only give me a penny a week so it took a long time to buy one. Paper representations of these infants climbed up a staircase, each step marking a penny paid towards their baptism. Mine was a girl, I coloured her skirt red and her jumper yellow, badly, though accidentally badly, so the slowness of her messy progress was a baleful reproach which lasted almost a year. I had no way of conveying this to my mother. Neither her inability to speed the process, or my ineptitude at colouring her in properly in the first place.

In the end, and after due payment of the 2/6d, I received a black and white picture of an African baby. I called her Catherine, and for years imagined this girl, growing up in Africa, named by me.

When I meet old friends and mention Black Babies they smile at the recollection of this long forgotten happening, and I am amazed, and say feebly that it was because of all that I became involved in politics. "Oh yes," they say, "I see what you mean." But they don't.

"You take it all so seriously," says my father, and I want to say, "oh was it all a joke?" But I don't.

No one is to blame for the chaos that informs the passage of my life. The nuns did not invent these processes, they were handed down through the institution of the Catholic Church during what now looks like a very evangelical period of its history. It is hard to imagine now that in those days exhibitions as large as today's 'Mind, Body, Spirit' convocations were held at venues like Olympia. Each stand extolled the virtues of a particular religious order handing out holy pictures, leaflets, recruiting literature, to encourage us to join one or another.

At home we recited the family rosary each night. Awkwardly kneeling on the floor of the dining room after supper.

The family that prays together stays together.

My father and I went to a stadium to hear the initiator of this scheme; an American priest, providing Catholics with an alternative to the Protestant evangelicals who were taking England by storm in the 1950's. We didn't need to join up, since we were already members. I wore a red tartan skirt and a yellow jumper and wished my name were Catherine, so chose it as my Confirmation name, and vowed to give it to the daughter I would have later.

If the analysis worked, it was accurate, we could change everything just by knowing what to do, but it doesn't so we can't. Some people go to the convents, and leave, and forget it all, at least that's what they say, and after all what else have we got to go on.

"The trouble with you is you think too much," says a friend, and I struggle to understand the meaning of that.

Which is, I suppose, exactly what she means.
Except I can't find the off switch.

The young men revolted by their mothers' bodies, glimpsed on beaches, in bathrooms, because they have been corrupted by pornographic imagery and cannot bear the ordinariness of real flesh and blood and bones, and the young Jewish woman who says "you're anti-semitic" and the young black woman who says "you are a racist" and I say "I don't know what you mean, I don't know what you mean, you're just a person, I don't think like that." and they say "Oh yes you do, you don't realise it, but you do. Listen to what you've said, you've said I'm 'just' a person, you've objectified me", and I say, "I don't mean that", "Aha", you say," but that's what you've just said", and I feel trapped and under the microscope of the thought police. I feel like someone in a psychiatric ward where first I have to say I'm wrong, or ill, or in need of treatment, and then I'll be treated and adjusted, and I feel two years old again, just looking, just feeling full of curiosity and no judgements, and you say the books of my childhood were racist and sexist and I say they were good, loving books, full of love, the story of Eppanimondous, a little black boy who foolishly misunderstood his mother and let the hens scratch up the peas she had carefully sown. You say it was about demonstrating that black people are less intelligent and I say no it wasn't it was about a piece of childhood life, because children do misunderstand and that Eppanimondous' mammy was very cross at first and then she got over being cross and held him in her big, enveloping arms and wiped away his tears and at the end of the book you see his happy smiling face and her happy smiling face and I knew to trust that it was alright for a child to misunderstand instructions.

And I say about Jewish people it was terrible. It was awful, to see your bodies piled high, to see your huge eyes staring out from behind the wire. I didn't understand 'Jewish'. You were people on the edge of destruction and it frightened me. What do you think it did but frighten me? Around me were the bomb sites, and I remember it all as black and white and grey and brown, it wasn't colour at all. My life wasn't colour and the pictures of your broken bodies weren't colour either, and my toys were made in brown wood by the man down the road, a little brown cart full of little brown bricks and a magic brown wood money box made like a chest of drawers. I put a penny in the top drawer, in a special circle made for the penny, and I shut the drawer and when I opened it again the penny had disappeared: and I went through the grey brown yellow streets of London to see 'Where the Rainbow Ends' and 'Peter Pan' and wished with all my heart for Tinkerbell not to die or you, and there were these people called Germans who were to blame for it all, or Germans called Hitler, who was dead I was glad to know, and so I do have a problem about Germans because they are very obedient which I was supposed to be, but not like that, which is very confusing, but anyway I haven't been very obedient, and I won't be obedient now about these things. I say the wrong word and people jump down my throat and say I mustn't say this or that . That when I say things it shows I don't understand and I think "Don't understand what? I understand we must love each other. What else is there to understand." I could make things with the bricks in my cart and I could put a penny in my money box and make it disappear. There are no words to describe trauma, there are no words to describe what happened to the small children of England, deemed fortunate to be so far away from it all, who took it in with their mothers milk.

I am talking about images,
mirages,
fears.
If we put a small child in a room and surround her with terrible images, pictures, tv, video,
images which are violent, obscene, depraved,
if the child hears sounds,
screams, wails, despairing howls,
and after that only the sound of her own cries,
and silence,
she will bang her head for comfort,
and the child grows up confused and muddled

what then is love

who is this God who exiles and punishes and
relishes the violent overthrow of enemies?
who is this God who says an eye for an eye and a tooth for a tooth?
who says you shall labour for the rest of your days and
in sorrow shall you bring forth children who is this parent who punishes children by death and destruction and an eternity of damnation and separation?
who is this person we worship
hanging,
tortured
on a wooden cross we have painstakingly constructed, and reconstructed,
hour upon hour
day upon day,
year
upon
year
for two millennia

consider the lilies of the field

the child grows up confused
is violence right or wrong?

always

sometimes
sometimes right
and sometimes wrong?
when is it right
and when is it wrong?

So I go to face these images
these fears.
The skeletal bodies. The eyes of the torturer.
The gaze of the victim.

I make the long journey across those killing grounds.
Normandy.
Flanders.

The cities solemn with memory.
Dresden.
Berlin.
Warsaw.
We stop at the border crossing for many hours.

The place where East meets West,

and it looks just like you'd think it would.

Seedy and surreptitious, and

Poland.

Poland is undergoing massive change. They were building a Macdonalds on the main street of the town I was staying in. Satellite TV abounds, CNN, Sky. 70's cartoons, Top Cat, Pixie and Dixie, all in English, though hardly anyone speaks English.

The local children wear sneakers and sweat shirts plastered with logos of American, Japanese owned, companies.

The average wage is half a dollar, or less, an hour. There are fruits and vegetables in the posh shops, at Western prices, but the people eat mashed potato and tinned meatballs. They use horses to plough their fields, though the crops are poor, due to the pollution. You can buy Kanlaschnikovs and goodness knows what else in the local market.

The people are cautious and closed. They would be. Just read their history. They love the Catholic Church and the US of A.

Near where I was staying is the bleakest town I have ever been in. Oswiciem where Auschwitz/Birkenau is situated.

Oswiciem, the town which contains the sins of the world. A few kilometres from the birthplace of Pope John Paul II.

Through the week on the tv screens in every bar, restaurant, hotel, we watched the unfolding horror of the execution of Nick Ingrams.

Just one example of hundreds on the death rows of America.

The horrors of the camps, the systematic torture and murder of millions of people is very nearly impossible to grasp. This event in Georgia, this systematic torture of one being, is easier to follow.

Just close your eyes and think about it. You are a Jew, a black, a caucasian, a homosexual, a gypsy, or you dissent from the status quo. You are the President of the United States, and according to the laws of your country, if what you do is considered unacceptable, you will be placed on Death Row, and never know when they are going to come for you.

And then one day another appeal fails, you've waited for this moment for twelve years and ....

I sat in this hotel in Poland and for two days heard over and over again how this execution would be carried out, other ways it could be carried out, what has happened to other victims, whether they accepted their fate calmly or hysterically. I was encouraged every step of the media way to put myself in his shoes. It has all got muddled in my mind by putting myself in the shoes of the victims of Auschwitz/ Birkenau, and there are shoes a plenty there to choose from. Where I struggled to understand the horrors of fifty years and more ago I had Ingrams in my mind, for sure this is murder post-Holocaust style.

Does that make it better or worse?

I daresay you kept him well fed during his twelve years, gave him good medical care if he was ill, had him examined by psychiatrists. I expect you checked his blood pressure and his heart. An ironic cruelty. Body and mind intact, fully functioning. I expect there was a tv and radio, a library. For all I know he was watching the same thing as me, except he would be watching himself, in those last dismal days.

Conditions at Auschwitz/Birkenau were not conducive to any illusion of virtual reality as perpetrated by the media moguls and their political allies.

I'd listen, like it or not, for I couldn't look, at the gruesome facts being detailed between commercial breaks advertising Coke, or trainers, or sleek cars, and watched the pinched Polish children impatient for Pixie and Dixie or Top Cat, and mercifully understanding nothing of what we were hearing.

The people of Eastern Europe know I have the privilege of a lifetime of comfort to enable my arrogant disdain of tawdry toys, cheap wares, junk food. I had a childhood and an adolescence and can afford to grow up and notice what's what.

My teenage son is into raves and the right to party. I danced the night away to the rhythms of jazz. I smoked dope, and of course inhaled. I was careless and irresponsible. I didn't sweep the streets or badger tourists to part with their money. I didn't have

to prostitute myself in national costume, or have my bottom pinched by rich Germans over sixty years of age.

I hitched around the continent of Western Europe escaping from the dreary bomb-cratered land of rationing and my parents inevitable need for certainty, and security, after the brutal interruption of their young lives which was World War Two.

The people of Eastern Europe are only now facing their former enemies, as coach loads of West German tourists re-invade their land, as truck loads of Russians display their spoils in the markets of their former colonies.

The mother of Nick Ingrams went for the American dream.

The land of instant gratification

Of the hand gun, the shot gun. The land of the Wizard of Oz and Reservoir Dogs.

Macarthy and Macdonalds.

Marilyn Monroe and O.J. Simpson.

In Eastern Europe no-one wants a past.

In modern America emotional accounts of the past fill the daytime tv screens.

At the World Monument at Birkenau people stand in inscrutable silence.

There are no words.

Of course America has no power. Just an illusion of power. And I want to say to the man, the most powerful man in the world, the President of the United States of America:

"If you step out of line you'll be out of a job. But oh what a marvellous moment that would be. When audiences all over the world hear a man who can throw a pebble in the pond, whose ripple will reach to the ends of the earth.

You have a chance to say what you stand for, a chance to be heard, a chance to be listened to. You have a chance to pick up that spliff and inhale deeply and.......

They said on that abominable Sky News that many Americans would be 'smiling with quiet satisfaction' at the murder of Nick Ingrams. I like to believe you didn't smile. I like to believe that along with many of your nation you still have enough imagination to abhor the barbarity of an execution carried out in your name. You are, after all, the Chief Executive, only the push of a button away from being the global executioner. I sleep less easy in my bed with your utterances and your finger poised.

There are no excuses. You belong to my generation. You heard John Lennon plead Imagine. You watched Apocalypse Now. You've seen the newsreels on the deathcamps and the effects of nuclear madness. You've seen what your gun crazed citizens will do. You are betraying a generation if you remain silent and you are betraying yourself. You are betraying the generation that refused the draft, that took the sneering comments of their fathers about being yellow, or commies, or wimps, or poofs, or all of those things, and more".

We're back in the land of cliché,
of soap opera,
the land of recall, where everything is possible in the moment,
and everything is regretted in retrospect
from a night's boozing to a night whoring
to a night's killing
tell it like it was,
or wasn't
tell it for the mess it was
say

I did that

and that

and that

look at the corpses and say

I did it because they told me to
because I have been taught to be obedient
because I love my parents and I want to please them

I did it because I can't say No

My nose drips,

my body aches with the long journey into inaccessible realms

The reality of my privilege strikes me again and again

a middle class woman
born in the middle of the twentieth century

the turning point

too young to know or

to be responsible.

and the part of my journey which really startled me was the comfort at Birkenau
when the world changed back
from technicolour
to black
and
white.

EPILOGUE

I have the images spread out in front of me
images of here
and there.

Here,
outside my room,
the scaffolding,
the graffiti,
the peeling posters,
the rotting mounds of rubbish.

There,

is a street of red brick buildings,
a car park, a hot dog stand, an hotel, a cafeteria, a bureau de change.
A flower bed has been planted,
a stiff row of pansies against a stone wall,

this is Auschwitz, and there,

a brief breeze bustles through the poplar trees
that remind me of the main gate at
Greenham Common

and the air vibrates to the exuberant song of countless birds making homes

in this vast arena, laid waste by human folly

crumbling concrete and powdered brick, rusty barbed wire, occasional lamps dangling from posts,

and everywhere the signs of restoration

remember, remember,
never forget